King George III:
England's Struggle to Keep America

Steve Roberts

CRABTREE
Publishing Company
www.crabtreebooks.com

Author: Steve Roberts
Publishing plan research and development:
  Sean Charlebois, Reagan Miller
  Crabtree Publishing Company
Editors: Leslie Jenkins, Janet Sweet, Lynn Peppas
Proofreader: Lisa Slone, Kelly McNiven
Editorial director: Kathy Middleton
Production coordinator: Shivi Sharma
Creative director: Amir Abbasi
Cover design: Samara Parent and Margaret Salter
Photo research: Nivisha Sinha
Maps: Paul Brinkdopke
Production coordinator and prepress technician: Samara Parent
Print coordinator: Katherine Berti

Written, developed, and produced by Planman Technologies

Cover: A portrait of King George III painted in 1781 by Thomas Gainsborough

Title page: (Left) The coronation of King George III by artist Joseph Kronheim; (Right) A portrait of King George III in 1799, by Sir William Beechey

Photographs and Reproductions
Front Cover: Wikimedia Commons / Royal Collection Trust © Her Majesty Queen Elizabeth II (b) / Shutterstock (t); Title Page: ©The Print Collector / Alamy / IndiaPicture; Universal / IndiaPicture; Table of Content: ©Old Paper Studios / Alamy / IndiaPicture; Library of Congress; ©The Print Collector / Alamy / IndiaPicture; Architect of the Capitol; ©Jeff Gilbert / Alamy / IndiaPicture; Library of Congress; Introduction: Library of Congress; Chapter 1: Library of Congress; Chapter 2: Library of Congress; Chapter 3: Library of Congress; Chapter 4: Library of Congress; Chapter 5: Library of Congress; Page 4: Library of Congress; Page 5: ©Old Paper Studios / Alamy / IndiaPicture; Page 11: Hulton Archive / Hulton Royals Collection / Getty Images; 13: ©19th era / Alamy / IndiaPicture; Page 14: Library of Congress; Page 15: Library of Congress; Page 16: Library of Congress; Page 17: ©The Print Collector / Alamy / IndiaPicture; Page 18: Library of Congress; Page 22: Library of Congress; Page 25: Everett / IndiaPicture (t); ©Timewatch Images / Alamy / IndiaPicture (b); Page 26: ©Ivy Close Images / Alamy / IndiaPicture; Page 27: Library of Congress; Page 29: Architect of the Capitol; Page 30: Library of Congress; Page 31: Library of Congress; Page 35: Library of Congress; Page 36: ©Jeff Gilbert / Alamy / IndiaPicture; Page 38: Library of Congress; Page 39: Universal / IndiaPicture;
(t = top, b = bottom, l = left, c= center, r = right, bkgd = background, fgd = foreground)

Library and Archives Canada Cataloguing in Publication

Roberts, Steven, 1955-
      King George III : England's struggle to keep America / Steve Roberts.

(Understanding the American Revolution)
Includes bibliographical references and index.
Issued also in electronic format.
ISBN 978-0-7787-0800-1 (bound).--ISBN 978-0-7787-0811-7 (pbk.)

      1. George III, King of Great Britain, 1738-1820--Juvenile literature.
2. Great Britain--History--George III, 1760-1820--Juvenile literature.
3. Great Britain--Kings and rulers--Biography--Juvenile literature.
4. United States--History--Revolution, 1775-1783--Campaigns--Juvenile literature. I. Title. II. Series: Understanding the American Revolution (St. Catharines, Ont.)

DA506.A2R63 2013   j941.07'3092   C2013-900234-0

Library of Congress Cataloging-in-Publication Data

Roberts, Steven, 1955-
   King George III : England's struggle to keep America / Steve Roberts.
      pages cm. -- (Understanding the American Revolution)
   Includes bibliographical references and index.
   ISBN 978-0-7787-0800-1 (reinforced library binding) -- ISBN 978-0-7787-0811-7 (pbk.) -- ISBN 978-1-4271-9079-6 (electronic pdf) -- ISBN 978-1-4271-9133-5 (electronic html)
1. George III, King of Great Britain, 1738-1820--Juvenile literature. 2. Great Britain--History--George III, 1760-1820--Juvenile literature. 3. Great Britain--Kings and rulers--Biography--Juvenile literature. 4. United States--History--Revolution, 1775-1783--Juvenile literature. I. Title.

   DA506.A2R63 2013
   941.07'3--dc23
                                                        2013000447

Crabtree Publishing Company

www.crabtreebooks.com   1-800-387-7650

Printed in Canada/022013/BF20130114

Published in Canada
Crabtree Publishing
616 Welland Ave.
St. Catharines, Ontario
L2M 5V6

Published in the United States
Crabtree Publishing
PMB 59051
350 Fifth Avenue, 59th Floor
New York, New York 10118

Published in the United Kingdom
Crabtree Publishing
Maritime House
Basin Road North, Hove
BN41 1WR

Published in Australia
Crabtree Publishing
3 Charles Street
Coburg North
VIC 3058

TABLE *of* CONTENTS

Introduction   4
Colonies in the New World | Ruler of an Empire

1   *The Making of a King*   8
Birth and Background | An Ordinary Child |
Prince of Wales | A Suitable Marriage

2   *The Early Reign of George III*   17
Long Live the King | The Seven Years' War |
Pitt and the King | The King's Troubles Begin |
A Royal Mess

3   *King George III and the American Revolution*   23
Taxing the Colonies | The American Reaction |
A Continuing Problem | The Road to War |
The Road to Independence | Fighting the Colonists |
Aftermath of the War

4   *The Later Reign of George III*   36
A Period of Peace | The French Revolution | The Irish
Rebellion | The Napoleonic Wars | The War of 1812

5   *The End of George III's Reign*   40
The Madness of King George | The King's Illness
Returns | The Final Years

Glossary, 42 | Timeline, 45 | Further Reading and Websites, 46 | Bibliography, 47 | Index, 48

Introduction

T he American Revolution, or the Revolutionary War, was a war between the American colonies and Great Britain. It raged from 1775 until 1783. It ended with the victory of the Americans over the British and the founding of the United States of America.

Colonies in the New World

Great Britain had fought long and hard to establish its colonies in America. The British finally gained complete control over its colonies after defeating the French in the Seven Years' War (also called the French and Indian War, 1756–1763). This war, however, left the British government in heavy **debt** and needing money.

The British considered the American colonies part of Britain and the Americans as British subjects. The British government, or Parliament, decided to raise taxes on the 13 American colonies to help pay for the war. Parliament also agreed not to expand its colonies any further into the American **frontier**.

The American colonists did not like these decisions. The colonists believed that, as British subjects, they should be **represented** in Parliament before any new taxes were **levied** on America. The phrase "no taxation without representation" became their protest **slogan**. The colonists also wanted the right to settle on land outside the existing colonies.

George III was the last king to rule over the American colonies. When he refused to hear the grievances against the British government, the colonists rose up against him.

4

The Americans **appealed** to Parliament but were rejected. They appealed all the way to the king of Great Britain, but the king also rejected their protests against the new taxes. When this happened, the Americans rose up against Britain, Parliament, and the king himself to fight for their independence.

Ruler of an Empire

The king of Great Britain during the late 1700s and early 1800s was King George III. Today he is remembered for two things: as the "king who lost America" and as the "**mad** king." This is somewhat unfair to King George. Although he lost the war with the American colonies and suffered from mental illness toward the end of his life, there was much more to the man.

The American Revolution lasted for eight years, but George III ruled Britain for almost 60 years. He was the third-longest **reigning monarch**, after Queen Victoria and the current monarch, Queen Elizabeth II. During his reign, he guided Britain through the Seven Years' War, fought off the French, and defeated Napoleon's efforts to take over Europe.

In his final years, George III was blind and **insane**. He lived in an **isolated** part of Windsor Castle, wandering its halls and wearing a velvet **dressing gown**.

He also argued at home with his own **prime ministers**, Parliament, and opposing political parties—the **Whigs** and the **Tories**. These groups often disagreed with the king—and each other—on how to run the **British Empire**. The truth is that they all shared the blame for losing America.

Under George III, Great Britain also became the **United Kingdom** and the most powerful empire in the world. The kingdom made great advances in science, industry, and agriculture during his reign.

To the Americans, he was a **tyrant** and a fool. But to the British people, he was a great king and a respected leader.

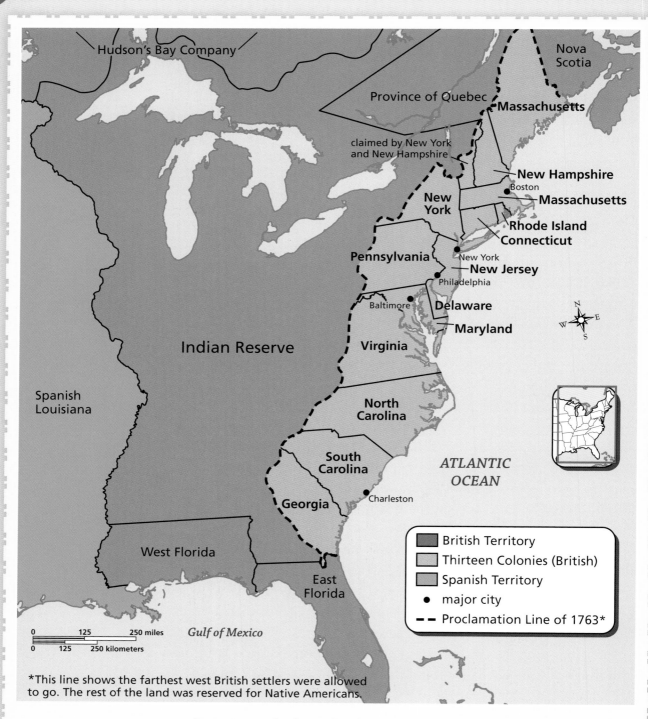

Hudson's Bay Company

Nova Scotia

Province of Quebec

Massachusetts

claimed by New York and New Hampshire

New Hampshire

Boston

Massachusetts

New York

Rhode Island
Connecticut

Pennsylvania

New York

New Jersey

Philadelphia

Baltimore

Delaware

Maryland

Indian Reserve

Spanish Louisiana

Virginia

North Carolina

South Carolina

ATLANTIC OCEAN

Georgia

Charleston

West Florida

East Florida

Gulf of Mexico

	British Territory
	Thirteen Colonies (British)
	Spanish Territory
●	major city
– –	Proclamation Line of 1763*

0   125   250 miles
0   125   250 kilometers

*This line shows the farthest west British settlers were allowed to go. The rest of the land was reserved for Native Americans.

North America before the Revolutionary War

Hudson's Bay Company

claimed by New York
and New Hampshire

claimed by New York
and Massachusetts

Massachusetts

New York

New Hampshire

Boston

Massachusetts

Rhode Island
Connecticut

Pennsylvania

New York

New Jersey

Philadelphia

Baltimore

Delaware

Spanish
Louisiana

Maryland

N
W · E
S

Virginia

claimed by
Virginia

**North
Carolina**

claimed by
North Carolina

*ATLANTIC
OCEAN*

claimed by
South Carolina

**South
Carolina**

claimed by Georgia

claimed by
United States
and Spain

Georgia

Charleston

	British Territory
	United States
	Spanish Territory
	territory claimed by two states
	territory claimed by U.S. and Spain
•	major city

0   125   250 miles
0   125   250 kilometers

Gulf of Mexico

Spanish
Florida

North America after the Revolutionary War

The Making of a King

Major Events

1738

June 4
George William Frederick born

1751

June 22
George's father dies, making 13-year-old George **heir** to British throne

1760

October 25
George's grandfather, King George II, dies

1761

September 8
George marries Princess Charlotte of Mecklenburg-Strelitz

September 22
George crowned King George III

George III was an unlikely British king. He almost died at birth, but he became one of Britain's longest ruling monarchs. He was from a German family, but he became one of the most British of kings.

Birth and Background

George III was born as George William Frederick on June 4, 1738, in London. He was the oldest son of Frederick, Prince of Wales, and Princess Augusta of Saxe-Gotha. George was born two months **premature**. Doctors thought he might not live, and he was immediately baptized. George, however, survived. He would live to rule Britain for almost 60 years.

George Frederick came from a long line of monarchs. His great-grandfather was George I. His grandfather was King George II. George Frederick's father, Frederick, was the oldest son of King George II and next in line to be king.

The House of Hanover

George was born into the royal family of a place called Hanover, a small kingdom in what is now Germany. In the past, the countries of Europe were ruled by royal families. George's family had married into Britain's royal family. When Queen Anne died in 1714, George's great-grandfather inherited the throne of Britain, even though he was from Germany. He became King George I. This was the beginning of a line of British rulers called the House of Hanover.

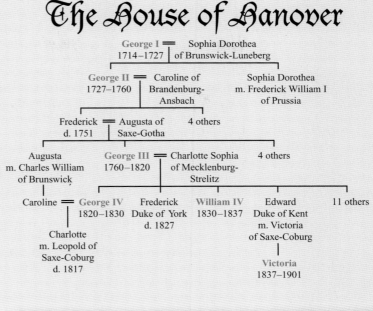

The House of Hanover

George I === Sophia Dorothea
1714–1727 of Brunswick-Luneberg

George II === Caroline of
1727–1760 Brandenburg-
Ansbach

Sophia Dorothea
m. Frederick William I
of Prussia

Frederick === Augusta of
d. 1751 Saxe-Gotha

4 others

Augusta
m. Charles William
of Brunswick

George III === Charlotte Sophia
1760–1820 of Mecklenburg-
Strelitz

4 others

Caroline === George IV
1820–1830

Frederick
Duke of York
d. 1827

William IV
1830–1837

Edward
Duke of Kent
m. Victoria
of Saxe-Coburg

11 others

Charlotte
m. Leopold of
Saxe-Coburg
d. 1817

Victoria
1837–1901

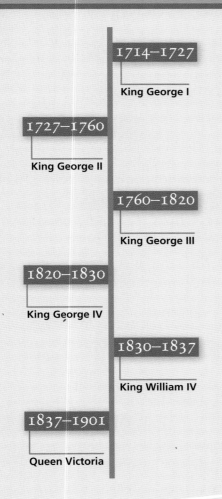

1714–1727
King George I

1727–1760
King George II

1760–1820
King George III

1820–1830
King George IV

1830–1837
King William IV

1837–1901
Queen Victoria

The House of Hanover ruled Britain for almost 200 years. The last of the Hanover royalty was Queen Victoria, the granddaughter of George III. She reigned Britain from 1837 to 1901. Queen Victoria's descendants are still the monarchs of Britain, but they use a different family name. The Royal Coat of Arms changed depending on who was king or queen and what parts of Europe were ruled by the British.

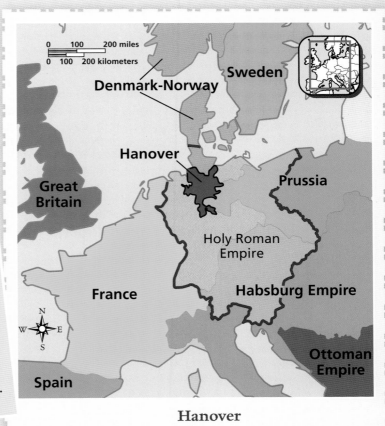

Hanover

THE GERMAN HANOVERS George's **ancestors** had all been born and raised in Hanover, in northern Germany. They were educated in Hanover, and German was their first language. They considered themselves primarily of Hanover **heritage**. Even George's father was raised in Hanover. He did not live in Britain until the age of 21, and he could not speak English. George's mother also came from a kingdom in Germany, called Saxe-Gotha.

The British never really accepted the first Hanoverian kings, George I and George II, as their rulers. They were viewed with suspicion by the British because they spoke English with a German accent and often visited or lived in Hanover.

George II was especially unpopular. He thought Hanover was better than Britain. He looked down on the British, from the way they dressed to the way they spoke. Whenever he complained against the British, he would do so in German. He made no effort to cover up his insulting behavior, which made him even more disliked. When George II went to the opera, the British people hissed at him.

His loyalty was to Hanover, and not to Britain. However, his grandson, George Frederick, would change all that.

A BRITISH HANOVER George was the first member of the House of Hanover to be born in Britain. He was the first to be educated in Britain and to speak English as his first language. He learned British history and British ways. During his lifetime, he never even visited Hanover.

He considered himself British first and foremost. He was very proud of his German heritage but made it his priority to protect the interests of Britain. For this, he was the first Hanoverian king to be accepted by the British people as one of their own.

> *Born and educated in this country, I glory in the name of Britain.*
> —George, in his speech to Parliament upon becoming king, 1761

An Ordinary Child

As a child, there was nothing special about George. He was slow to develop, possibly due to his premature birth. He was considered **immature** for his age, both emotionally and **intellectually**. By some accounts, he was a poor reader and could not read properly until the age of 11. By other accounts, he was able to read and write in both English and German by the age of eight. Generally, however, he was an average child of average ability.

George was very shy and reserved, but also very stubborn. He made up for his lack of intelligence with hard work and **determination**. From an early age, he took his role as a member of the royal family very seriously.

Princess Augusta of Saxe-Gotha, George's mother

Childhood Influences

As a member of the royal family, George led a sheltered life. His early life was dominated by his family. The strongest influence on him was his mother, Princess Augusta. She was a **devoted** mother but also thought to be too overprotective.

George's father, Frederick, was a good father and took a strong interest in his son's upbringing and education. George also had a brother, Edward, who was one year younger. The young princes were raised and educated together.

One of George's childhood friends was Frederick North, who was six years older than George. Frederick and George would act in plays put on by the royal family. Frederick North's title was the Earl of Guilford, or Lord North. He later became George III's prime minister during the American Revolution.

> *Bow to the Prince, my son, address him as Your Royal Highness. If you play a game with him, he must win. . . If you play your part well, you may in time get a sinecure post [easy but profitable job].*
>
> —Advice given to Frederick North by his parents on how to play with the future King George

A Tragic Turn

In order to act more British, George's father took a great interest in **cricket**, a popular game similar to baseball. One day while playing cricket, he was hit in the chest with a ball. The injury formed an **abscess** on his lung, and on June 22, 1751, George's father died at the age of 44. His father's sudden death was a shock to George, and it had a huge impact on his future.

Prince of Wales

The Prince of Wales is the title given to the oldest son of the king or queen of Britain. The prince is the next in line for the throne when the current king or queen dies. As a result of his father's death, George became the Prince of Wales and heir to the throne. George was 12 years old.

When his grandfather, George II, died, George would become king. George II was already 67—considered an advanced age—and could die at any time.

A Royal Education

George was raised to be the next king. He did not go to school. He was taught at home by private **tutors**. He worked hard to prepare himself to serve his country and his people.

> *His person is tall and full of dignity, his countenance florid [red-cheeked] and good natured, his manner graceful and obliging, he expresses no warmth or resentment against anybody.*
>
> —Horace Walpole, describing young George, 1761

George took lessons in Latin, French, German, and Greek. He studied algebra, history, and astronomy, as well as physics and chemistry. Because he might lead an army one day, he was also taught military strategy and the science of **fortification**.

As the future king, George was given lessons in manners and social graces expected of his position in **society**. So that he would be well-rounded in his abilities, he learned how to play the **harpsichord** and the flute. He learned how to **fence**, dance, and ride horseback.

Young George's daily schedule was busy. This is what a typical day looked like for him:

The Hours for the Prince

- To get up at 7.
- At 8 to read with Mr. Scot [a tutor] till 9, and he to stay with them till the Doctor [another tutor] comes.
- The Doctor to stay from 9 till 11.
- From 11 to 12, Mr. Fung [another tutor].
- From 12 to half an hour past 12, Ruperti; but Mr. Fung to remain there.
- Then to the Play hour till 3.
- At 3 Dinner.
- Three times a week at half an hour past 4, Denoyer [the dancing master] comes.
- At 5, Mr. Fung till half an hour past 6.
- At half an hour past 6 till 8, Mr. Scot.
- At 8, Supper.
- Between 9 and 10 in Bed.

George was judged by his teachers to have a strong heart but a weak mind. He was weak in some areas, but he showed promise in others. He took a strong interest in astronomy and agriculture, and showed signs of great taste in the arts. The letters that George wrote show that he was intelligent but frightened, unhappy, and **insecure** about his future.

The Earl of Bute

George's mother, Augusta, was aware of his feelings. In 1755, when George was 16, she got rid of all his tutors and had her close friend, John Stuart, take over his education. John Stuart came from a Scottish **noble** family. His title was the Earl of Bute, or simply Bute.

George immediately bonded with Bute, and Bute became a father figure in George's life. He became George's teacher, friend, and closest adviser. Rather than teach him about math, history, and science, Bute taught George about **philosophy**, **diplomacy**, and the art of **politics** and power. George trusted Bute and tried to win his approval on everything. Later, when George became king, Bute became his prime minister.

> **What Do You Think?**
>
> How is George's schedule different from most 13-year-olds' daily schedules? Why do you think George was frightened, unhappy, and unsure about his future?

John Stuart, the Earl of Bute

> *In what a pretty pickle I should be in a future day if I had not your sagacious [wise] counsel.*
>
> —George, in a letter to Bute, 1758

A Suitable Marriage

In 1759, when George was 20, he confessed to Bute that he was **depressed**. He wanted a wife. In particular, he was interested in Lady Sarah Lennox, the beautiful sister of the Duke of Richmond. He wished to marry her.

He wrote to Bute for permission to marry Lady Lennox. Bute refused. He told George that if he was to be king, he could not marry one of his own subjects. He would have to marry a princess from another royal family. This made George even more unhappy.

> *I am born for the happiness or misery of a great nation and consequently must act in contrary [opposite] to my passions.*
>
> —George in a letter to Bute on being denied permission to marry Lady Lennox, c. 1760

Princess Charlotte

Bute arranged for George to be married to Princess Charlotte of Mecklenburg-Strelitz. She was from a small kingdom in Germany. She was a highly intelligent and attractive young woman about the same age as George. The first time George and Charlotte met was on their wedding day.

As royal marriages go, this one turned out to be unusually successful. George was married to Charlotte for 57 years, and they had 15 children. He was a very **devoted** husband and father, and Charlotte stood by him during his most difficult years.

Princess Charlotte of Mecklenburg-Strelitz. George wanted to marry Lady Lennox but was forced to marry Princess Charlotte. She turned out to be a perfect match.

A Man of Culture

During his reign, George III was well-loved by many and hated by some. Yet all who knew the king agreed that he was a man of culture. He came to power during the **Enlightenment**, a movement in Europe that valued reason, scientific exploration, and intellectual curiosity. George III was eager to advance the Enlightenment in Britain.

When George took the throne in 1760, there was no royal library—only small collections of books in some of the royal homes. In 1763, he decided to create a library worthy of the royal family. He purchased the large personal library of a wealthy **diplomat**, and he sent agents to buy important book collections in Britain and Europe. By his death in 1820, the Royal Library contained 65,000 books, a **Gutenberg Bible**, and many maps. It was open to all **scholars**, even the American revolutionary John Adams, who visited the Royal Library after the American Revolution.

George was mocked in the press as "Farmer George," but the nickname was later used as a term of affection by the people.

One of George's scientific instruments was an orrery. It demonstrated how the earth and moon revolve around the sun.

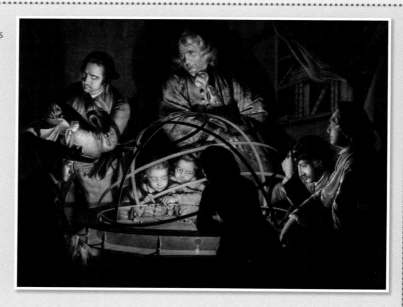

In 1768, George III founded the Royal Academy of Art to showcase the talents of British artists and **architects**. An art school was established there as well. Every year from 1769 until today, the Academy has held a summer **exhibition** of British artists. Not even World War I or II stopped the Royal Academy of Art from staging this annual show.

George III was an enthusiastic student of agriculture. He was given the nickname "Farmer George." He was especially interested in improving the quality of farm animals. **Cartoonists** made fun of him for growing crops and letting sheep graze on the grounds of the royal estates. But later in his life, his love of gardening and farming made the British citizens feel that George was a man of the people.

As a boy, George III was the first British prince ever to be taught science, or natural philosophy as it was called at the time. He was fascinated by the many scientific discoveries that were taking place in astronomy. He even had his own **observatory**. George also funded the largest telescope ever to be built at that time, a 40-foot telescope used by the astronomer William Herschel. Herschel had discovered the seventh planet in our solar system and named it George's Star in honor of George III, but the planet's name was later changed to Uranus. George III collected many mathematical and scientific instruments, and today you can still see his collection at the Science Museum in London.

The 60-year reign of George III was marked by ongoing wars with France and the loss of the American colonies. But his cultural **legacy** lives on in the Royal Academy of Art, the Royal Library, and in the work of the many British scientists, artists, and thinkers who **flourished** under his rule.

The Early Reign of George III

George III became king of Britain during a time of great **turmoil**. The Seven Years' War—or French and Indian War—with France was in its fifth year, and the British government could not agree on how to run the country.

Long Live the King

George's grandfather, George II, died suddenly on October 25, 1760. This made George the king. He was 22 years old. George Frederick was officially crowned King George III on September 22, 1761.

George III was welcomed as the new king. For the first time since the House of Hanover assumed the throne almost 50 years earlier, the people felt they had a truly British king. He was young and handsome. People hoped he would be a strong king and unite the arguing groups in the British government.

Major Events

1760

October 25
George's grandfather, George II, dies

1761

September 22
George is crowned King George III

October
William Pitt resigns

1762

May 26
The Duke of Newcastle resigns; Bute becomes prime minister

1763

February 10
Peace of Paris treaty signed with France

October 7
George III issues the Royal Proclamation of 1763

Coronation of George III

When George III became king, he found the government in a mess. The two parties in the government, the Whigs and the Tories, constantly fought with each other and even among themselves. As a result, it often took the government a long time to make important decisions. At times, it seemed as if no one was in charge.

The British Government

The British government is called Parliament. The Whigs and the Tories met in Parliament to argue over matters affecting the country. They disagreed about everything, from how to run the country to who should run it. One of the main issues they argued about was the war with France.

The head of the British government was the prime minister. The prime minister was determined by whichever party had the most representatives in Parliament, similar to the Speaker of the House in the United States today. The prime minister chose his own ministers, or cabinet, and they made the important decisions. The prime minister when George III became king was the Duke of Newcastle. His top minister was William Pitt the Elder.

The King Asserts His Power

When George first took the throne, the king had very little power. Parliament had taken power from the monarch under George I and George II. William Pitt basically ruled the country.

George was taught that it was the duty of the king to serve his country. He was determined to **assert** his royal authority and restore the people's confidence in their king. He also wanted to get rid of Pitt as he believed that Pitt was **corrupt**.

George's first decision as king was to **appoint** his own cabinet. He picked his old teacher, the Earl of Bute, as his top minister and adviser. Then he set out to end the Seven Years' War.

People in the War

William Pitt the Elder

Although the Duke of Newcastle was prime minister, William Pitt the Elder ran the government during the Seven Years' War. Pitt worked closely with Newcastle on Britain's military strategies and later became prime minister from 1766–1768. His policies toward the American colonies helped lead to the American Revolutionary War. His title now is William Pitt the Elder to distinguish him from his son, William Pitt the Younger, who also became prime minister. The city of Pittsburgh in Pennsylvania is named after William Pitt the Elder.

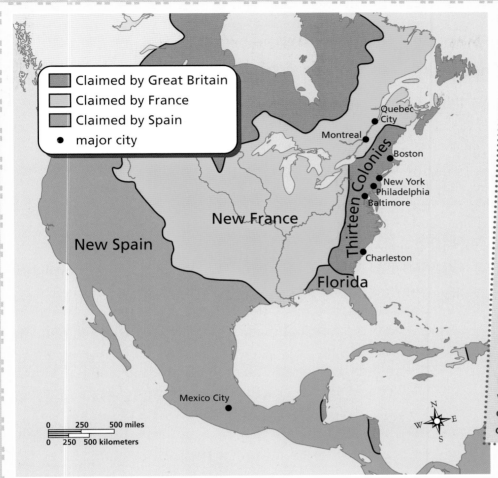

Legend:
- Claimed by Great Britain
- Claimed by France
- Claimed by Spain
- ● major city

Quebec City
Montreal
Boston
New York
Philadelphia
Baltimore
Charleston

Thirteen Colonies

New France

New Spain

Florida

Mexico City

0 250 500 miles
0 250 500 kilometers

European Claims in North America

The Seven Years' War

The French and the British had fought each other for centuries over control of Europe. During the Seven Years' War (1756–1763), they fought each other over control of overseas colonies, especially in North America. Both countries wanted colonies as a source of land, wealth, and resources.

A World War

The Seven Years' War was not fought only by the French and the British. Several other European countries also had overseas colonies to protect. Russia, Austria, and Spain sided with the French. Portugal and Prussia sided with the British. In North America, Native Americans fought on both sides.

The war was not limited to North America. Fighting also took place in Europe, Central America, Africa, India, and the Philippines. Because of the scope of the war, the Seven Years' War has sometimes been thought of as the first actual world war.

Pitt and the King

By 1762, Britain was winning the war. It had taken over most of the French colonies in North America and almost completely destroyed the French navy. The British government, however, discovered that Spain had made a secret agreement to join the war in support of France.

Pitt was in favor of continuing the war. He had a plan to attack the Spanish navy and its colonies before Spain could join the war. The king opposed Pitt's plan. Although Britain had mostly defeated the French, the war had become very costly. Many in the government agreed with the king and wanted to end the war.

With so many people against him, Pitt resigned. A few months later, the Duke of Newcastle resigned as prime minister.

George chose his old teacher, the Earl of Bute, to replace Newcastle as prime minister. George III was now effectively in charge of the government. George told Bute to **negotiate** a treaty with France to end the war.

The Peace of Paris

On February 10, 1763, Britain signed a treaty called the Peace of Paris with France, ending the Seven Years' War. Britain now controlled most of what had been French territory to the Mississippi River, including all of the 13 American colonies and most of Canada. Under the treaty, France was allowed to keep some of its territory if they would agree to peace and not go to war again.

The King's Troubles Begin

George III was popular when he first took the throne. Once he became king and began to rule, he quickly made enemies. Some of the decisions he made were **criticized** by the government, the British people, and the American colonists.

Many members of Parliament, especially the Whigs, were opposed to the king asserting his royal authority. The Whigs thought Parliament should run the government and the king should have no say. Many people were opposed to the Treaty of Paris. George III soon learned that trying to serve Britain as king was a thankless job.

The Royal Proclamation of 1763

After the Treaty of Paris was signed, George wanted to protect the colonies in America. They were still under threat of attack from the Spanish, the French, and Native Americans. Later that same year, on October 7, George signed the Royal Proclamation of 1763.

The Royal Proclamation set strict limits on the western border of the British colonies. The purpose was to prevent another war. If anyone crossed the border and attacked the colonies, it would be considered an act of war. The colonists were also not allowed to cross the border so they would not **provoke** a war with someone else.

Many of the American colonists were against the Proclamation of 1763. They thought it limited their freedom. They wanted the right to settle western land. They were far from Britain and did not think they should have to do whatever the king said.

A Royal Mess

When George III became king, the government disagreed about almost everything. They did, however, agree about one thing—defeating the French. Fighting the French brought the Parliament, the political parties, the British people, and the king together.

George took over and ended the war in Britain's favor. Now that the war was over and the French were defeated, the country could not agree again. George needed to find something else on which they all could agree. He found it in paying for the Seven Years' War.

Paying for the War

The Seven Years' War had been fought to protect the British colonies and had cost a fortune. Now that the colonies were secure, George had to find a way to pay for the war. There was one thing he found on which everyone in Britain could agree. The colonies should have to help pay for the cost of the war and the cost of maintaining the colonies. This set off a series of events that led to the American Revolution.

AN UNSTABLE GOVERNMENT

During the first ten years of George III's reign, Britain had seven different prime ministers. George fought constantly with Parliament over who should be prime minister. After signing the Treaty of Paris, Bute was so unpopular that he resigned. He was followed by George Grenville, who was chosen by Parliament. George did not get along with Grenville and fired him after one year. Grenville was followed by Lord Rockingham, who was also fired by George after one year. Rockingham was followed by George's old enemy, William Pitt, who died a year later. After Pitt, the Duke of Grafton became prime minister but resigned after a year. He was finally replaced by Lord North, George's childhood playmate. Lord North would serve as prime minister for 12 years and help steer George III through the American Revolution.

Lord North

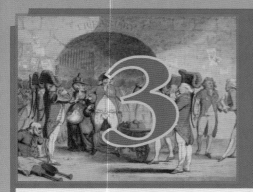

King George III and the American Revolution

3

Britain had defeated France in the Seven Years' War and added new colonies to its empire. Now George III needed to protect those colonies. He soon found himself at war again. This time it was not with France. It was with the colonists themselves.

Taxing the Colonies

With the addition of France's colonies, Britain had a lot more territory to defend, which would cost a lot more money. There were 10,000 soldiers in the colonies that needed to be **armed**, clothed, and fed. Britain had also borrowed money to fight the Seven Years' War and needed to pay it back.

The British government needed to raise taxes. In Britain, the people were already paying high taxes. In America, the colonists paid very little in taxes, even though they were British subjects. The British Parliament, prime minister, and people agreed that the colonists should pay more in taxes for their own upkeep. George III agreed. In 1764, Parliament passed the Sugar Act, taxing sugar and molasses. Then in 1765, Parliament passed the Quartering Act, requiring the colonists to house and feed the British army.

Major Events

1764
Sugar Act passed

1765
Stamp Act passed
Quartering Act passed

1766
Sugar and Stamp Acts repealed

1767
Townshend Acts passed

1770
Townshend Acts repealed;
Lord North becomes prime minister

1773
Tea Act passed

December 16
Boston Tea Party

1774
Coercive Acts passed

Major Events

1775
April 19
American
Revolution begins

1776
July 4
Continental
Congress passes the
Declaration of
Independence

1778
France enters the
war on the side of
America

1781
October 19
British are defeated
at the Battle of
Yorktown

1783
The Treaty of Paris
ends the American
Revolution;
William Pitt the
Younger becomes
prime minister

The Stamp Act

In 1765, Parliament passed the Stamp Act. The act said that all legal papers, such as land deeds, wills, and licenses, had to have an official government stamp on it. A tax was charged for the use of every stamp.

The British did not think the stamp tax was unfair. People in Britain already paid a stamp tax. The amount of tax for Americans was much less than what the British paid. Besides, the taxes would go to pay for the British troops stationed in America and not to Britain itself.

The American Reaction

Some of the leaders of the colonists were against paying these taxes. Even though the taxes were low, they increased the cost of doing business for many people. There was, however, one major reason the Americans **protested**.

No Taxation without Representation

Most of the Americans were not against paying taxes or against helping take care of the soldiers. What they opposed was paying taxes without having a voice in the British government's decisions. Even though they were British citizens, they had no one to represent them in Parliament. The Americans' **rallying cry** was "no taxation without representation." They feared that the British government would make more demands on the colonists without them having the right or power to stop it.

 What Do You Know!

TAXES
The government provides different types of services for its citizens that they, as individuals, cannot pay for themselves. Among the many services the government provides are:

- national defense
- police departments
- fire departments
- schools
- courts
- roads
- parks
- libraries

The government raises money to pay for these services. The way it raises money is by collecting taxes. Taxes are small amounts of money, or fees, that people pay for being part of society. Taxes are placed on things like buying and selling goods, owning property, and earning an income. Individuals pay taxes so that the government can pay for the things that benefit all of society.

Boycotting the British

The Americans sent **petitions** to Parliament with their demands, but Parliament rejected them. The Americans decided they needed to take stronger action. Leaders from several of the colonies met in New York to discuss what to do. They decided to **boycott**—or refuse to buy—British **goods**. The British **economy** relied heavily on the sale of products to America. The boycott reduced **trade** between Britain and America so much that British **merchants** complained to Parliament.

The King Takes Action

Parliament and the prime minister could not agree on what to do. The king was asked to step forward and make a decision. George was considered a peacemaker for having ended the Seven Years' War.

Stamps like these were attached to documents to show the Stamp Act tax had been paid.

George decided to take the side of the colonists. He fired the prime minister and appointed a new one. Then he convinced Parliament to **repeal** the Sugar Act and the Stamp Act. This ended the taxing of the colonists. Parliament also ended the Quartering Act.

The Americans were overjoyed. The colonists did not blame King George for the taxes. They blamed the British Parliament. Parliament had passed the taxes, and George had ended them. King George was now a hero in America. He was so popular that the colonists built a statue of him in New York.

Ministers in Parliament

A Continuing Problem

George's problems were not over. He still needed to raise money to pay for the upkeep of the colonies. He chose Charles Townshend, who knew a lot about **finance**, to head the British **treasury** and solve the problem.

> *The issue is whether Parliament can legally take money out of our pockets without our consent.*
>
> —John Dickenson, Letters from a Farmer in Pennsylvania, c. 1767

The Townshend Acts

Though most protesters were peaceful, other colonists acted out with violence. In some cases, they damaged government offices or even attacked tax collectors.

Townshend came up with a new idea that was not much different from the old one. Americans would still have to pay taxes. But they would only have to pay taxes on things that they could not make themselves and needed to get from Britain. In 1767, Parliament passed the Townshend Acts, taxing glass, paint, oil, lead, tea, and other products.

The Second Boycott

The Americans were not happy about this. As they saw it, the British Parliament was still telling them what to do and not giving them any say about it. Even worse, Parliament was taxing more goods than before.

The Americans again protested and boycotted the taxes, but the results were the same. Trade between Britain and America suffered. British merchants asked Parliament to reconsider the taxes. Again, George fired the prime minister and urged Parliament to end the taxes. This time George chose his childhood playmate, Lord North, as the new prime minister.

In 1770, Parliament repealed the Townshend Acts. The colonists again claimed victory. Parliament, however, made one important **exception** to repealing the taxes.

The Road to War

Parliament did not think it should give up its right completely to tax the colonies. George agreed. It was a matter of **principle**. At the king's request, Parliament kept one tax—the tax on tea.

There must always be one tax to keep up the right [to tax the American colonies].

—George III to Parliament

The Tea Act

Although the Americans still objected to paying any tax, there were no major problems at first. Americans loved to drink tea and were willing to put up with the tax. Many American merchants also made their living shipping tea. Others got around the tax by **smuggling** tea into the colonies from other countries.

In 1773, Parliament passed the Tea Act. The biggest supplier of tea, and one of the most powerful British businesses, was the British East India Company (EIC). The Tea Act was passed to help them fix their financial problems. It allowed the company to ship tea directly to America rather than going through American merchants. This would put a lot of American merchants out of business, and Americans would still have to pay taxes on the tea.

During the Boston Tea Party, the colonists disguised themselves as Mohawk warriors. They did this because it was a crime to destroy someone else's property, and they could go to jail if they were identified.

The Boston Tea Party

This time the Americans did not react peacefully. On the night of December 16, 1773, a group of colonists secretly boarded an EIC ship and threw hundreds of chests of tea overboard. The event became known as the Boston Tea Party.

This was a very serious action. It was one thing to protest taxes, send petitions to Parliament, or refuse to buy British goods. It was another thing to destroy the property of a powerful British company. It was a criminal offense.

> *This destruction of the tea is so bold, so daring, so firm, . . . It must have such an important and lasting result that I can't help considering it a turning point in history.*
>
> —John Adams in his diary the day after the Boston Tea Party

Until the Boston Tea Party, the British had been divided on how to treat the colonists. Some members of Parliament thought the colonists should be given more freedom. Others thought not. The British people and the king could not decide whose side to take. The Boston Tea Party united all sides in Britain against the colonists. The colonists had gone too far. This time the British would not give in to them.

The Coercive Acts

In 1774, Parliament quickly passed the Boston Port Act, the Massachusetts Government Act, the Justice Act, the new Quartering Act, and other measures. Among other things, these new acts closed the port of Boston and required the colonists to feed and house British soldiers again. In Britain, these were called the Coercive Acts. In America, they were called the **Intolerable** Acts.

The Continental Congress

As many Americans saw it, Parliament only passed these acts to punish the colonists. Representatives from each of the colonies met in Philadelphia to discuss what to do. This was the meeting of the First Continental Congress.

The Continental Congress decided to ban all British goods from the colonies. They also drew up a list of demands. Among them was that Parliament repeal the Coercive Acts.

The War Begins

The British government rejected the Americans' demands. Instead, it sent troops to take over the city of Boston. On April 19, 1775, a battle broke out between the colonial **militia** and British troops in the towns of Lexington and Concord. These were the first shots fired in the American Revolutionary War.

The Battles of Lexington and Concord began when British troops went in search of weapons hidden by the Massachusetts militia. The militiamen were tipped off that the British were coming by the famous midnight ride of Paul Revere.

The Road to Independence

Representatives of the colonies quickly met again in the Second Continental Congress. They decided to organize their own army—the Continental Army—to fight the British army. The Second Continental Congress, however, also decided to make one last effort to avoid an all-out war.

The Olive Branch Petition

The Americans did not blame George III for their problems with Britain at first. They blamed the British government. It was Parliament and the prime minister that had passed the taxes. In the past, King George had stepped in on their behalf and made Parliament repeal the taxes. The colonists had even built a statue to honor him.

The Second Continental Congress drew up a petition asking the king to intervene on their behalf again. It was called the Olive Branch Petition because the olive branch is a symbol of peace.

The King's Reaction

George refused to even look at the petition. He believed it was his duty to support Parliament and not side with the Americans. He also believed that, as British subjects, the colonists' duty was to support their mother country.

George also saw the rebelling colonists as troublemakers. He declared that the Americans "were engaged in open and avowed rebellion" and that the rebels were traitors. He called upon all those loyal to the crown to put down the rebellion.

> *He has abdicated [removed] Government here. . . . He has plundered our seas, ravaged our Coasts, burnt our towns, and destroyed the lives of our people.*
>
> —The Declaration of Independence, 1776, about George III

Declaring Independence

George's declaration changed the minds of many Americans. They had still thought of themselves as British and George III as their king. Now they no longer saw their enemy as Parliament or the prime minister. Their enemy was the king himself.

The Continental Congress met again on July 4, 1776, and issued the Declaration of Independence. The document charged George III with violating their rights and called him a "tyrant." The Declaration said that the American colonies were no longer part of Britain, and that they would rule themselves. Their new name was the United States of America.

The Declaration of Independence was read aloud in town squares across the colonies. When it was read in New York City, the crowd tore down the statue of George III they had put up when he repealed the Stamp Act.

Fighting the Colonists

King George was determined to defeat the rebels and restore British authority in the colonies. He would attack the rebels both by land and by sea. He had good reason to think the British would win.

A painting shows contrast between the Redcoats and Patriots

The British Advantages

The British navy was the most powerful in the world and controlled the Atlantic Ocean. British ships could easily strike anywhere along the American coast. The Americans had almost no navy.

George also had the most powerful army in the world. His officers were experienced and educated in military **tactics**. His soldiers were well-armed and well-trained. The Continental Army was small and had few experienced officers or well-trained troops.

The British Disadvantages

The British also faced some challenges. Fighting to keep the American colonies would be expensive. Also, as a result of winning the Seven Years' War, the British colonies were much larger than before. The British army would have a hard time taking over and occupying so much territory.

> *The die is cast. The colonies must either submit [give up] or triumph. I do not wish to come to severe measures, but we must not retreat.*
>
> —George III in a letter to Lord North, 1775

Early Victories

At first the war went well for George. In August 1776, only one month after the Americans declared independence, the British army defeated the Continental Army in the Battle of Brooklyn, the first major battle of the war.

Soon after, the British army took over New York City, followed by New Jersey and Philadelphia. The British army defeated the Americans' attempt to invade Canada by beating them at Fort Ticonderoga. The fort housed British supplies and cannons. Ticonderoga's strategic location near Boston would allow the British army to attack the colonists from behind.

🌠 **What Do You Think?**

Which side would you have chosen? Would you have been a Patriot and rebelled against the king? Or would you have been a Loyalist, wanting to keep your life the same? Why?

People in the War
Loyalists

Not all of the colonists were against British rule and wanted independence. In fact, most of the colonists did not at first support the rebels and just wanted to be left in peace. Those who supported the rebels were called **Patriots**.

A large number of colonists supported Britain and King George. They were called **Loyalists**. In some parts of the country, more colonists joined the British side than the Patriot side.

Among the Loyalists were many Africans and African Americans. Slavery was common in the colonies. The British government promised to set free any slaves who fought on Britain's side. Many slaves joined with the British to fight for their own freedom against the colonists.

When the British lost the war, many black Loyalists who could not leave the United States were sold back into slavery. The British, however, kept their promise. Many of the black Loyalists moved to Canada or Britain, where they were free.

The Tide Turns

The Continental Army led by George Washington turned out to be tougher and smarter than King George had expected. Because of America's size, the British army and navy were spread too far out. The Americans were also accustomed to the rough and rugged countryside. The British were accustomed to fighting on streets and in cities. In September and October 1777, the Americans defeated a British army in Saratoga, New York.

This was a turning point. The powerful British army no longer seemed **invincible**. The Americans were encouraged. To make matters worse, Britain would soon face its old enemy, France, again.

After the Americans beat the British at Saratoga, the French believed the Americans had a chance of winning the war. In March 1778, France entered the war on the side of America. Soon after, Spain—another old enemy of Britain—joined the war in support of America. Britain no longer had the advantage in the war.

By 1780, the British began to tire of the war. Many thought Britain could no longer win and did not want another long, costly war like the Seven Years' War.

George insisted Britain must keep fighting. He was worried that if America won, other British colonies in Ireland, Africa, and India might also rebel and demand their independence. He was also concerned that it would make Britain look weak to its enemies in Europe. George still hoped for victory until the Battle of Yorktown.

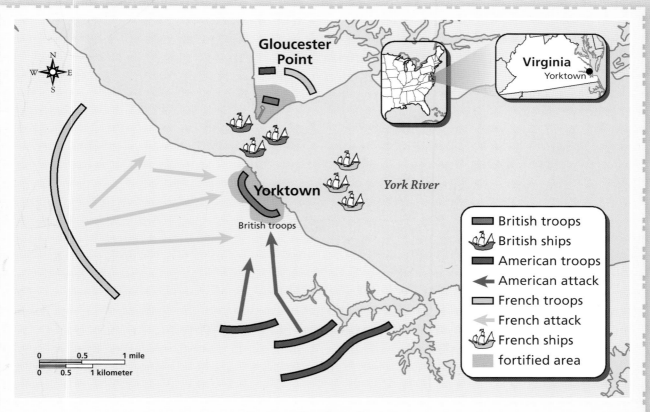

The Battle of Yorktown

The End of the War

In September 1781, the British army in Yorktown, Virginia, was surrounded on land by a combined army of American and French forces. The only escape was by sea. In October, a fleet of French ships arrived, trapping the British navy. On October 19, British General Lord Cornwallis **surrendered**.

When word of the surrender at Yorktown reached George, he knew the war was lost. Parliament voted to put an end to the fighting and make peace with the Americans. On September 3, 1783, Britain signed the Treaty of Paris, formally ending the Revolutionary War.

> " *America is lost!*
> —King George III,
> c. 1781

Aftermath of the War

The war was over, but George's problems were not. Britain was shaken by the loss of its American colonies. There were questions about who was to blame and how to handle the peace.

A Change of Government

Now that the war was over, Lord North was allowed to resign as Prime minister. He had been George's prime minister for 12 years. A new government had to be formed for a new era.

The government was split between the Tories, who supported the king, and the Whigs, who opposed him. The Whigs formed the new government.

The Whigs chose Lord Rockingham as prime minister. Rockingham, however, died soon after. He was replaced by the Earl of Shelburne, who made the peace treaty with America. Parliament thought he gave away too much to the Americans, so he was forced to resign. Shelburne was replaced by the Duke of Portland.

Portland ran the government with the support of Charles James Fox. George III hated Fox. Fox was not only a Whig, but a man of bad character. Worst of all, Fox had turned George's own son—the Prince of Wales—against him. George's son had joined the Whig party, publicly opposing his father.

The King's Minister

George found a way to fire Portland and Fox, and to get Parliament to let him choose his own prime minister. He chose William Pitt the Younger. He was the son of William Pitt the Elder, one of George's earlier prime ministers. The older Pitt had been a Whig and an opponent of the king. The younger Pitt had become a Tory and a supporter of the king.

Pitt was only 24 years old when George appointed him. He was the youngest prime minister in British history. He also became one of the greatest prime ministers. He served George III for the next 20 years.

Making Peace with America

No one took the loss of the American colonies harder than George did. He felt like he had personally let down his country. He was the king who had lost the colonies. George even offered to step down as King over it.

George did learn to accept the loss. In 1785, he met with John Adams. Adams was one of the founding fathers of America and one of George's greatest enemies. Adams visited George as the first American ambassador to Britain. It marked the beginning of the close friendship Britain eventually **forged** with America.

John Adams was America's first ambassador to Britain and the second president of the United States.

> " I was the last to consent to the separation [of Britain and the colonies]; but the separation having been made and having become inevitable [unavoidable], I have always said, as I say now, that I would be the first to meet the friendship of the United States as an independent power. "
>
> —George III to John Adams, 1785

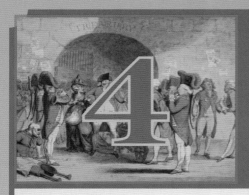

The Later Reign of George III

Major Events

1786

August 2
First assassination attempt on King George

1789

July 14
The French Revolution begins

1793

February 1
France declares war on Britain

1798

The Irish Rebellion

1800

Act of Union unites Britain and Ireland, creating the United Kingdom of Great Britain and Ireland

May 15
Second assassination attempt on King George

Britain had lost the war with the colonies but was at peace. The peace would not last long. Britain would soon have problems with its old enemy, France, as well as with the Americans again.

A Period of Peace

The war was over and William Pitt the Younger was prime minister. Britain was at peace and had a stable government. Pitt was George's own choice for Prime minister, and they got along well. The country began to **prosper**.

A Popular King

George was in middle age and in good health. He was a happily married man and loyal to his family and country. With the country at peace, he could spend more time on his interests in books, science, and agriculture.

Royal Academy of Art which George III founded in 1768.

George had been a slow learner as a child, but he became one of the most educated rulers in Europe. He wrote booklets on how to improve agriculture. He started the Royal Library and the Royal Academy of Art. Under his rule, Britain produced some of its greatest writers.

Trouble Ahead

The American Revolution, however, would continue to cause problems for George in ways he did not expect. The American Revolution **inspired** other revolutions that affected Britain. The first was the French Revolution. The second was the Irish Rebellion.

The French Revolution

Inspired by the American Revolution, on July 14, 1789, the French people overthrew the king of France. They later executed the king. This frightened all of the other rulers in Europe. They were afraid their own people would also revolt and kill them.

George, however, was not bothered. He thought the king of France got exactly what he deserved for supporting the American Revolution. But he still had reason to worry.

War with Revolutionary France

The new government in France wanted to overthrow all of the other monarchs of Europe. In 1793, France declared war on Britain and attacked. Britain was no longer fighting France over the colonies in America, but was now fighting for its own **survival**.

The British fought off the French for several years. They finally won the war when the British navy beat the French navy. In 1802, the French and the British signed a peace agreement to end the war.

George did not think the peace agreement would last. The leader of the French army was Napoleon Bonaparte. George thought he would come back again. He was right.

> ❝
> *Do you know what I call this peace? An experimental peace, for it is nothing else.*
>
> —George III on signing the peace agreement with France in 1802
> ❞

Major Events

1801

October 1
End of the war with France

1803

Renewed war with France

1807

The Slave Trade Act abolishes slavery

1812–1814

War of 1812 between Britain and the United States

1815

Napoleon defeated at the Battle of Waterloo

The Irish Rebellion

Inspired by both the American and French revolutions, Ireland rose up against Britain in 1798. Ireland was also a British colony and wanted its own independence. The Irish fought the British with help from the French.

The Act of Union

The Irish and French forces were beaten by the British. In 1800, Britain made a peace agreement with Ireland called the Act of Union. In the Act of Union, the Irish agreed to stop fighting the British if they could have representation in Parliament. The country was renamed from the Kingdom of Great Britain to the United Kingdom of Great Britain and Ireland.

> *We are here in daily expectation that Bonaparte will attempt his threatened invasion. Should his troops effect a landing, I shall certainly put myself at the head of mine, and my other armed subjects, to repel them.*
>
> —George III in a letter to Bishop Hurd, 1803

The Napoleonic Wars

In 1803, Napoleon had crowned himself Emperor of France and was **determined** to take over the world. He planned to invade Britain. George was determined to stop him.

Defending Britain

George met with Pitt and the Parliament, and they decided to declare war on Napoleon. George rallied the people, who **volunteered** by the thousands to fight off the French. George personally inspected the troops and promised to lead them into battle.

This cartoon shows George III studying Napoleon in the palm of his hand. Napoleon Bonaparte, the Emperor of France, tried to conquer all of Europe. He was finally defeated at the Battle of Waterloo.

Defeating Napoleon

George and his forces fought off Napoleon for several years by land and by sea. Napoleon's navy was defeated at the Battle of Trafalgar by Admiral Nelson. His army was defeated by General Wellington at the Battle of Waterloo. Britain was safe again.

The War of 1812

Peace did not last. Britain got into another war with the United States. It was called the War of 1812.

Some British sailors had been **deserting** to join the American navy. British ships began to stop all American ships to find British deserters. Sometimes they would kidnap American sailors into the British navy.

The United States and Britain declared war on each other. But after two years of fighting, neither side had gained much ground. They both agreed to the other's demands and made peace in 1814.

God Save the King!

George became a new symbol of national pride. He was no longer seen as "the king who lost America," but as the king who saved Britain from France. But there were still some people who would do him harm.

At two different times, someone tried to **assassinate** King George. On August 6, 1786, a woman named Margaret Nicholson lunged at the king with a knife. The woman was stopped, and the king was not harmed. She was mentally unwell and sent to a home for the mentally ill.

On May 15, 1800, George went to see a play at the Drury Lane Theatre. A man named James Hadfield stood on a box and fired two shots at him. The bullets barely missed him, and the man was quickly caught. The king was calm about his brush with death. George insisted the play should go on and even fell asleep during it. Hadfield was tried in court for treason, but he was also found to be mentally ill.

> *The poor creature is mad; do not hurt her, she has not hurt me.*
>
> —George III after he was attacked by Margaret Nicholson in 1786

Assassination attempt on King George

Ending the Slave Trade

George III made many other **contributions** to British history. During his reign, the Slave Trade Act of 1807 ended slavery in the British colonies. This began the long process of ending slavery around the world.

The End of George III's Reign

5

Major Events

1788
George's first bout of mental illness

1810
George's mental illness permanently returns

1811
Regency Act passed

1818
November 17
George's wife, Queen Charlotte, dies

1820
January 29
King George III dies

In America, George III is remembered as the king during the Revolution. In Britain, he is remembered for losing the colonies but saving Britain from France. Sadly, there is one other thing for which he is famous—as the king who lost his mind.

The Madness of King George

In the summer of 1788, George began to act strangely. His body would shake and he could not stop talking. According to one story, he was seen talking to a tree, which he thought was the king of Prussia.

The King Falls Ill

Later that year, on November 5, 1788, George suddenly attacked someone during a dinner party, grabbing the person and slamming his head against a wall. The king spoke nonsense, his eyes were red, and he was foaming at the mouth. It was clear that the king had lost his **sanity**.

Doctors back then knew very little about mental illness. They did not know what caused it or how to treat it. They believed things like "evil **humours**" had invaded his body.

His doctors tried to talk the king into being sane again with lectures and threats. They put him in a **strait jacket** to restrain him. He was chained to an iron chair made especially for him. His body was covered with strong medications to draw out the evil humours.

The King Recovers

The doctors did not know if the king would ever get better and thought he might die. The king, however, slowly **recovered**. After a few months, he was well enough to go out in public again. What had happened to him was a complete mystery.

The King's Illness Returns

Twelve years later, in 1810, George began to act strangely again. His illness had returned. People hoped he would recover like he did before. That was not to be.

By 1811, it was clear that George would never recover. Parliament had a special meeting and passed the Regency Act of 1811. It allowed George's oldest son, the Prince of Wales, to act for the king. When George died, his son would become the next king, George IV.

The Final Years

Even though George did not recover and no longer ruled for himself, he lived for another ten years. Queen Charlotte cared for him until she died in 1818.

The Death of the King

By the end of his life, George was blind and had lost most of his hearing. Because of his state of mind, he could not understand that his wife had died or even that he was king. In his last few weeks, he was unable to walk.

He died at Windsor Castle on January 29, 1820. He was 81 years old, a very old age at the time. He had ruled Britain for almost 60 years.

Remembering the King

A great funeral was held for the king, and his death was **mourned** by the country. He was remembered as a king who was a well-meaning man and steered his country through hard times. He became a symbol of Britain, both good and bad.

THE CAUSE OF THE KING'S ILLNESS

What caused George's madness remains a mystery. A few years ago, scientists took some samples of the king's hair and studied them. They found high levels of the chemical **arsenic**. In large amounts, arsenic can affect the brain and make someone act just like the king did.

Where the arsenic came from is also a mystery. Some people think the king might have been poisoned on purpose. Other people point out that arsenic was a common element used in make-up at the time. It was common for members of royalty, both men and women, to wear make-up. The king might have been exposed to too much of it.

It is also possible that George had been born with an illness called porphyria. Porphyria is a blood disease that poisons the nervous system and causes the type of problems the king had. The king might have suffered from a severe case of the disease.

GLOSSARY

abscess an inflamed area of the body surrounded by pus

ancestors the relatives from whom a person descended; parents, grandparents, great-grandparents, etc

appeal to try and have a decision changed by a higher authority

appoint to name to an office

architect the designer of a building

armed bearing a weapon

arsenic a poisonous chemical; in the 1700s, small doses were used to make white cosmetics

assassinate to kill by surprise, often a public official with a political motive

assert to state strongly or make known

boycott to refuse to buy, usually goods

British Empire the territory ruled by Great Britain; included the American colonies, Canada, Australia, New Zealand, Hong Kong, India, South Africa, among others

cartoonist an artist who draws cartoons; during the 1700s, cartoonists often made social commentary in their drawings

contributions things with a positive impact, often social

corrupt dishonest; often governments or government officials

cricket a team ball game with two sides of 11 players each; players score runs by running between two wickets

criticize to judge, usually negatively

debt borrowed money or funds

depressed extended period of sadness

deserting leaving without permission, usually from the military

determination commitment to complete a task or fulfil a promise

determined committed to bearing and completing the task at hand

diplomacy negotiations building or maintaining a relationship between or among two or more countries

diplomat one who negotiates in the relationships between or among nations

dressing gown robe

economy the exchange of goods, services, and money

element (chemistry) the building blocks of everything; oxygen, carbon, mercury are examples

Enlightenment an intellectual movement of the late 1700s, which emphasized reason and science over religion or tradition

exception one thing that is different from the rest of the category

exhibition a public display or showing

fence to practice fencing, a sword-fighting sport

finance the study of money and banking

flourish to thrive or do well

forged build, especially through a difficult circumstance

fortification a wall or other construction, specifically to protect an army or military position

frontier the edge of the settled world

goods products or manufactured items

Gutenberg Bible a copy of the Bible produced by the Gutenberg printing press, the first moveable type printing press; one of the first printed books in the world

harpsichord a musical instrument similar to a piano except that the strings are plucked instead of hammered in a piano

heir one who inherits or receives a title, land, or wealth upon the death of the holder

heritage a person's ancestry or parentage; a person's ethnic background

humours (archaic) the four fluids that were believed to determine a person's mood and personality; choler, blood, melancholy, and phlegm were the four humours

immature acting younger than one's age

insanity an unsteady state of mind; unable to be reasonable or sensible

insecure not steady or confident

inspire move to action; cause an event to occur, especially resembling a previous event

intellectually having to do with the mind or higher thinking

intolerable unable to be tolerated; insufferable

invincible unable to be beaten

isolated separated from the rest

legacy the impact an individual leaves behind

levied charged a tax; the passing of a tax in the legislature

Loyalist one who sided with Great Britain in the Revolutionary War, wanted the colonies to remain in the British Empire

mad (archaic) insane or unstable in the mind

merchant someone who buys or sells goods for profit

militia a military unit made up of citizen soldiers; usually saved for emergencies

monarch the hereditary, or family-inherited, ruler of a nation or people

mourn to grieve a loss, especially the death of a family member

negotiate to bargain or barter; especially in diplomacy

noble from a high-status family

observatory a scientific institution made for the study of the natural world or sky

Patriot one who desired independence for the American colonies from Great Britain

petition a formal letter, usually to a government or official, asking for an action or law

philosophy the study of the beliefs, attitudes, and concepts of a group or individual

politics the leading of governments or societies; competition for power in the government

premature before the proper time; in children, describes a child before the full term of pregnancy

prime minister the leader of the legislature and government; usually chosen from the majority party

principle values or ideas to which people are committed

prosper to grow, thrive, or do well

protested objected to or publically demonstrated against a law or policy

provoke to incite or cause a violent action

rallying cry a phrase or slogan used to inspire action or belief

recover to become well again

reigning being in charge at the time; ruling

repeal to cancel, usually a law

represented to stand for the beliefs or interests of a group in a political system

sanity mental ability or competence

scholars experts or researchers in a particular area

slogan a phrase used to inspire action or belief

smuggling the act of illegally importing goods, usually to avoid paying a tax

society the system of community or communities; often operate with a shared set of views and values

strait jacket a jacket which ties the arms; used to restrain a person from harming themselves or another

surrender to give up or lay down arms

survival continuing or living longer than expected or longer than another

tactics the ways of directing troops in battle

Tory (Britain) a member of the Conservative Party; generally loyal to the monarch and traditional government

trade the exchange of goods, services, and money; often between or among nations

treasury the agency of government responsible for financial or economic decisions

turmoil a confused or mixed up state of affairs

tutors private teachers

tyrant a individual who rules on personal decisions rather than the will of the people; an all-powerful ruler

United Kingdom The United Kingdom of Great Britain and Ireland; the country made up of the union of England, Scotland, Wales, and Ireland from 1800 until 1922; preceeded by the Kingdom of Great Britain (England, Wales, Scotland) from 1707 to 1800; from 1922 to present, the United Kingdom of Great Britain and Northern Ireland

volunteer to expressing willingness (to fight, for example) without being required

Whig (Britain) a member of a political faction that wanted more power in Parliament and less power for the monarch (constitutional monarchy)

TIMELINE

1738	*June 4*	George William Frederick is born
1751	*June 22*	George's father dies, making George heir to the throne
1760	*October 25*	George's grandfather, King George II, dies
1761	*September 8*	George marries Princess Charlotte of Mecklenburg-Strelitz
	September 22	George is crowned King George III
	October	William Pitt resigns as prime minister
1762	*May 26*	Duke of Newcastle resigns as prime minister; Bute becomes prime minister
1763	*February 10*	The Peace of Paris is signed with France
	October 7	George III issues the Royal Proclamation of 1763
1764–1765		The Sugar Act, the Stamp Act, and the Quartering Act are passed
1766		The Sugar and Stamp Acts are repealed
1767		The Townshend Acts are passed
1770		The Townshend Acts are repealed; Lord North becomes prime minister
1773		The Tea Act is passed
	December 16	Boston Tea Party
1774		The Coercive Acts are passed
1775	*April 19*	Battles of Lexington and Concord; the American Revolution begins
1776	*July 4*	Continental Congress passes the Declaration of Independence
1778		France enters the war on the side of America
1781	*October 19*	British are defeated at the Battle of Yorktown
1783		The Treaty of Paris ends the American Revolution; William Pitt the Younger becomes prime minister
1786	*August 2*	First assassination attempt on King George
1788		George's first bout of mental illness
1789	*July 14*	The French Revolution begins
1793	*February 1*	France declares war on Britain
1798		The Irish Rebellion
1800		The Act of Union unites Britain and Ireland, creating the United Kingdom
	May 15	Second assassination attempt on King George
1801	*October 1*	End of the war with France
1803		Renewed war with France
1807		The Slave Trade Act abolishes slavery
1810		George's mental illness permanently returns
1811		The Regency Act is passed
1812–1814		War of 1812 between Britain and the United States
1815		Napoleon defeated at the Battle of Waterloo
1818	*November 17*	George's wife, Queen Charlotte, dies
1820	*January 29*	King George III dies

FURTHER READING AND WEBSITES

Books

Aloian, Molly. *George Washington: Hero of the American Revolution.* Crabtree Publishing Company, 2013.

Aloian, Molly. *Phillis Wheatley: Poet of the Revolutionary Era.* Crabtree Publishing Company, 2013.

Brooks, Phillip. *King George III: America's Enemy.* Franklin Watts, 2009.

Clarke, Gordon. *Significant Battles of the American Revolution.* Crabtree Publishing Company, 2013.

Cocca, Lisa Colozza. *Marquis de Lafayette: Fighting for America's Freedom.* Crabtree Publishing Company, 2013.

Fritz, Jean and Margot Tomes. *Can't You Make Them Behave, King George?* Puffin, 1996.

Mason, Helen. *Life on the Homefront during the American Revolution.* Crabtree Publishing Company, 2013.

Perritano, John. *The Causes of the American Revolution.* Crabtree Publishing Company, 2013.

Perritano, John. *The Outcome of the American Revolution.* Crabtree Publishing Company, 2013.

Schanzer, Rosalyn. *George vs. George: The American Revolution As Seen from Both Sides.* National Geographic Children's Books, 2007.

Websites

"Arsenic and King George III." *Neuroscience for Kids.*
http://faculty.washington.edu/chudler/george.html

"George III (r. 1760–1820)." *The Official Website of the British Monarchy.*
http://www.royal.gov.uk/Historyofthe Monarchy/KingsandQueensoftheUnited Kingdom/TheHanoverians/GeorgeIII.aspx

"George III Biography." *The Biography Channel.*
http://www.thebiographychannel.co.uk/biographies/george-III.html

"George III." *BBC History.*
http://www.bbc.co.uk/history/historic_figures/george_iii_king.shtml

"House of Hanover Family Tree." *Royal Family History.*
http://www.britroyals.com/Hanover.htm

"King George III (1760–1820)." *Royal Family History.*
http://www.britroyals.com/kings.asp?id=george3

BIBLIOGRAPHY

Books

Gaines, Ann Graham. *King George III*. Chelsea House Publishers, 2000.

Hibbert, Christopher. *George III: A Personal History*. Basic Books, 1998.

Ayling, Stanley. *George the Third*. Alfred A. Knopf, 1972.

Fraser, Antonia, ed. *The Lives of the Kings and Queens of England*. University of California Press, 1998.

Fraser, Antonia, ed, and John Clarke. *The Houses of Hanover and Saxe-Coburgh-Gotha*. University of California Press, 2000.

Websites

"George III (king of Great Britain)." *Encyclopedia Britannica*. **www.britannica.com/EBchecked/topic/230026/George-III#toc2635**

"George III (r. 1760–1820)." *The Official Website of the British Monarchy*. **www.royal.gov.uk/historyofthemonarchy/kingsandqueensoftheunitedkingdom/the hanoverians/georgeiii.aspx**

"King George III (1760–1820)." *Royal Family History*. **http://www.britroyals.com/kings.asp?id=george3**

Cannon, John. "George III." *The Oxford Companion to British History*. **www.encyclopedia.com/topic/George_III.aspx**

"George III." *Encyclopedia of World Biography*. **http://www.encyclopedia.com/topic/George_III.aspx#2**

Baack, Ben. "The Economics of the American Revolutionary War." *Economic History Association*. **eh.net/encyclopedia/article/baack.war.revolutionary.us**

"Black Loyalists." *The Loyalist Pages*. **http://www.americanrevolution.org/black loyalists.html**

Library of Congress Prints and Photographs Online Catalog. **www.loc.gov/**

INDEX

Act of Union (1800), 38
Adams, John, 15, 27, 35
American colonies, 4, 16, 20, 21, 23–34
American Revolution, 4–5
Anne, Queen of Great Britain, 8
Army, Continental, 29, 31, 34
Augusta of Saxe-Gotha, Princess, 8, 9, 11, 13

Bonaparte, Napoleon 5, 37, 38
Boston Tea Party, 27–28
British Empire, 5
Brooklyn, Battle of, 31
Bute, John Stuart, Earl of, 13, 18, 22

Canada, 20, 21, 32
Charlotte of Mecklenburg-Strelitz, Princess, 9, 14, 41
Congress, Continental, 28, 29, 30
Cornwallis, General Lord Charles, 34

Declaration of Independence, 30

East India Company (British), 27
Edward, Duke of York, Prince (brother of George III), 11
Elizabeth II, Queen of the United Kingdom, 5
Enlightenment, 15

Fox, Charles James, 34–35
France, 5, 16, 18, 21, 22, 23, 32–33, 36, 37
Frederick, Prince of Wales (father of George III), 8, 9, 11, 12
French Revolution, 37
frontier, American, 4, 21

George I (great-grandfather of George III), 8, 9, 10
George II (grandfather of George III), 8, 9, 10, 12, 17
George III (George William Frederick), King of Great Britain,
    agriculture, interest in, 13, 16, 36
    ancestry, 8, 9, 10
    and American colonies, 4–5, 23, 25, 29–30, 34
    and Parliament, 5, 18, 21, 22
    and prime ministers, 11, 13, 18, 22, 25, 26, 34, 35
    arts, interest in, 13, 16
    assassination attempts on, 39
    astronomy, interest in, 13, 16
    birth, 8

childhood, 8, 11–13
children of, 9, 14, 34
coronation of, 17
death, 41
education, 11, 12–13
family tree, 9
Hanoverian heritage, 8, 9, 10
marriage, 14
mental illness, 5, 40–41
George IV, King of the United Kingdom (son of George III), 9, 34, 41
Grafton, Augustus FitzRoy, Duke of, 22
Grenville, George, 22

Hadfield, James, 39
Hanover, 8, 9, 10
Hanover, House of, 8, 9, 17

Intolerable (Coercive) Acts, 28
Irish Rebellion, 38

Lennox, Lady Sarah, 13
Lexington and Concord, Battles of, 29
London, 8
Loyalists, 32

mental illness, 40–41

Native Americans, 20, 21
navy, British, 31, 33
Newcastle, Thomas Pelham-Holles, Duke of, 18, 20
Nicholson, Margaret, 39
North, Frederick, Earl of Guilford, Lord, 11, 26, 34

Olive Branch Petition, 29

Parliament, 4–5, 18, 23, 24, 25, 26, 27, 28, 29, 30, 41
Patriots, 32
Peace of Paris (1763), 21
Pitt, William, the Elder, 18, 20
Pitt, William, the Younger, 35, 36
porphyria, 41
Portland, William Cavendish-Bentinck, Duke of, 34–35
prime minister. See
    • Bute, John Stuart, Earl of.
    • Grafton, Augustus FitzRoy, Duke of.
    • Grenville, George.
    • Newcastle, Thomas Pelham-Holles, Duke of.

    • North, Frederick, Earl of Guilford, Lord.
    • Pitt, William, the Elder.
    • Pitt, William, the Younger.
    • Portland, William Cavendish-Bentinck, Duke of.
    • Rockingham, Charles Watson-Wentworth, Lord.
    • Shelburne, William Petty-FitzMaurice, Earl of.
Proclamation of 1763, 21

Quartering Act, 23, 25

Rockingham, Charles Watson-Wentworth, Lord, 22, 34
Royal Academy of Art, 16, 36
Royal Library, 15, 36
Saratoga, 32–33

Seven Years' War (French and Indian War), 4, 5, 17, 20–21, 22, 23, 25, 31, 33
Shelburne, William Petty-FitzMaurice, Earl of, 34
Slave Trade Act (1807), 39
Spain, 20, 21
Stamp Act, 23–25
Sugar Act, 23, 25, 30

taxes, 4, 23, 24
Tea Act, 27
Tories, 5, 17, 21, 34
Townshend Acts, 26
Townshend, Charles, 26
Treaty of Paris (1783), 34

United Kingdom (of Great Britain and Ireland), 5, 38
United States, 4, 35, 36

Victoria, Queen of the United Kingdom (granddaughter of George III), 5, 9

Wales, Prince of (title), 12
Waterloo, Battle of, 38
Whigs, 5, 17, 21, 34
William IV, King of the United Kingdom (son of George III), 9
Windsor Castle, 5, 41

Yorktown, Battle of, 33–34